This book is dedicated to James Wals[...] ; an old friend who has often experienced [...] and sometimes in the day. I must confess t[...] ips, but his success has been that he's take.. .... a smile.

Louis Peck Jr. watches over the grave of his ancestor buried in Exeter, Rhode Island in 1892. Mercy Brown was thought to be a vampire. She was dug up, her heart removed and cooked, then eaten—this was the cure for vampirism a hundred years ago.   ISBN 0-916787-15-x

COVER PHOTO

This picture was taken on the evening of May 24, 1980 from Quincy Park in Beverly, Massachusetts during a severe thunder storm, by Norman "Dugie" Russell. Beverly and Salem were in total darkness because of a shorted out generator at the Salem Power Plant. The center lightning bolt is striking Bakers Island and the left bolt, Little Misery Island.

- 1 -

INTRODUCTION

What is it that you fear in the dead of the night? Would a growl or a hiss from a dark corner of your bedroom frighten you? How about loud, hideous laughter from some inhuman form standing at the foot of your bed? That's what finally drove Steve Barsanti out of his wits in the chapter titled "The Boogeyman of Beggerly". Would coming face to face with an orange-eyed blob with long arms and legs and with no nose or lips, unnerve you at all? It caused a few twittering hearts in Dover, Massachusetts—and what about Bigfoot? Would you like to meet up with a Yeti while camping or hiking in the northern New England woods? If so, the chapter on Sasquatch will tell you where to go to find these big hairy fellows. If you're prone to witches, vampires and werewolves, this book will also let you know where they hang out. Also haunted islands and ships at sea off our coast, will beckon you to explore the depths of the unknown and the supernatural.

These are all true stories of strange incidents and bizarre encounters right here in our New England backyard. The reason for relating them to you is not just to provide you with some unusual history, but to give you a chill or two, and maybe make you think twice about turning off the light before you go to bed tonight. Are there really things out there hiding in the shadows, real and supernatural, that are ready to pounce on us the moment we let down our guard? You think not. Read on my friend, but then explain to me why you keep looking over your shoulder.

Bob Cahill

The haunted GRAMPUS, former CAN DO, that sank in the Blizzard of-78, is ashore for repairs at Salem. Photo by Craig Burnham.

I
Spooky Spirits Of The Sea

Throughout history certain vessels have gained evil reputations, sometimes with just cause, but usually because some accident or mishap seemed to justify a superstitious sailor dubbing the vessel *"jinxed,"* or a *"hoodoo"* or *"voodoo"* ship. If a crewman suffers some adversity aboard a certain ship, he and his friends may refuse to sail on her again. Or, if an otherwise perfectly designed vessel rolls fretfully in a severe storm, she may be damned forever because her crew is unwilling to sail on her again. Word of a cursed, haunted, or jinxed vessel, spreads from seaport to seaport, until the shipowner is unable to gather a crew anywhere. If a shipyard worker is severely injured or killed while building a ship, or if there is an accident or death at the launching of a ship, that ship is considered cursed before she even hits the water. Although such seaside superstitions have moderated somewhat over the years, they are almost as prevalent today as they were one hundred years ago.

Such a voodoo ship strains at her anchorage only a few hundred yards from my own home in Salem, Massachusetts. She is the 48-foot GRAMPUS, owned by my neighbor Craig Burnham. He recently invited me to take a cruise up the Maine coast on his vessel, and I refused. I was willing to board her and even spend a day on her, but I wouldn't sleep aboard the GRAMPUS, and there are others who feel as I do. Some would refuse to even board her, and the sailors and fishermen of nearby Gloucester have informed Craig Burnham that they do not want to see the GRAMPUS in the harbor, so Craig avoids that port. Craig says that he was a little spooked when he first owned the GRAMPUS, because of her tragic history. But all those *"chilling feelings"* have left him now, and he sleeps aboard her *"without a second thought."*

I first boarded the GRAMPUS while she was docked in Gloucester Harbor, back in June of 1973. She was a happy ship then. Frank Quirk, an old friend and a Gloucester pilot, had recently purchased her as a pilot-boat, and had changed her name to CAN DO. Frank had been a Seabee during World War II, and the Seabee warcry *"Can Do,"* was one that Frank Quirk lived by. He and I had both been professional divers during the early days of scuba diving in New England, and I learned in the early 1950's that Frank was a bit of a daredevil, who could do just about everything and would attempt anything. Frank and his wife Audrey were living aboard the CAN DO, and they were as happy as a couple could be. Less than five years later, February, 1978, I was in bed, high on a hill at Salem Hospital, with a panoramic view of Salem Harbor, awaiting open-heart surgery after a heart-attack and stroke. If the snowstorm outside hadn't blinded my view, I might have witnessed the terrible tragedy of the CAN DO and the death of my friend Frank Quirk and his crew.

My brother Jim, who later became Salem's Harbor Master, called me to ask if I could see the 628-foot oil tanker, GLOBAL HOPE anchored off Coney Island Ledge in Salem Sound. Word was that she was dragging her anchor and in danger of hitting the ledge. The wind was howling outside my hospital window and the thick flakes were flying. I told my brother that I couldn't see a thing—it was the afternoon of February 6, 1978, and the Great Blizzard of '78 was underway. As Jim and I were talking, the GLOBAL HOPE, carrying 2.1 million gallons of oil, smashed into Coney Island Ledge. *"I am in dangerous place,"* the Greek captain of the tanker shouted over the radio to Warren Andrews, Salem's shipping control radio operator. *"My ship has gone aground on the ledge, the hull is broken, my engine room is flooding."* Radio contact with the distressed tanker was cut off immediately as the engine room flooded, shutting off the ship's power. Andrews notified the Coast Guard station at Gloucester. They sent out a 41-foot patrol boat, but she was forced back once outside Gloucester Harbor because of heavy seas. The Coast Guard then sent out a more seaworthy vessel, a 44-foot surfboat, built for heavy seas, but her crew was inexperienced and her compass wasn't working right. The blizzard was now at full fury, 60-mile an hour winds and 20-foot seas with zero visibility. The 44-footer would normally make an emergency run from Gloucester to Salem Harbor in half an hour, but when that time period had expired, the skipper of the surfboat radioed Coast Guard headquarters: *"We are lost,"* announced the skipper, *"negative radar, negative fathometer and no binnacle light."* The Coast Guard Chief, Mike Parady at Gloucester Headquarters, ordered the skipper to give up the rescue attempt of the GLOBAL HOPE and attempt to find Beverly Harbor.

Frank Quirk, with four of his crewmen, was listening to the Coast Guard conversation on his radio aboard the CAN DO, which was snuggled into the inner harbor at Gloucester. *"You want me to take a shot at it?"* Frank asked Parady over the radio. *"I don't know if anyone is really in danger aboard the tanker, Frank,"* Parady replied. *"My concern now is getting my 44-footer to safety...He's totally disoriented at this time....If at all possible, I'd appreciate it if you'd head over that way."*

"Even with a compass and radar," said Quirk, *"you wouldn't believe how bad it is out there, but we'll give it a shot, Mike."*

The CAN DO headed out of Gloucester Harbor and pointed her steel hull into the wild seas. Frank kept up radio contact with the Coast Guard and with Salem Harbor's radio operator, Warren Andrews, well into the night. A giant wave hit the CAN DO, smashing in her windshield and slicing Quirk's arm. *"We're taking in water through the windshield....The radar is down and everything else is down,"* reported a weary voice. *"Pilot boat CAN DO, three miles off Salem Harbor...Radar missing...Trying to keep warm. Three of the boys are below in sleeping bags....A mattress in the window....feeling weak...loss of blood...."* and those were the last words Warren Andrews heard from Frank Quirk.

The Blizzard continued through February 7th, and on the morning of the 8th, two bodies were found off Nahant and two more washed onto a Marblehead beach. One was Frank Quirk. The skipper and crew of the GLOBAL HOPE were safe and sound, although the vessel was high and dry on Coney Island; and the Coast Guard surfboat, although slightly damaged, made it safely into Beverly Harbor. Only the CAN DO, the ship sent out to rescue the others, was missing. She was found underwater a few days later by scuba divers off Tinkers Island, Marblehead, and the fifth body was found in her engine room. One of the scuba divers who salvaged the CAN DO was Craig Burnham. He towed her into Salem's North River, hoisted her onto the ways and began repairing her stoved-in hull and cabin.

No, I won't spend a night aboard the GRAMPUS, the former CAN DO, and I don't know if my reluctance is due to being a friend of Frank Quirk's, or that I'm superstitious. *"You sure you've never had a strange or eerie experience aboard the GRAMPUS since you fixed her up?"* I asked Burnham, a quiet, sober young man who eyed me quizically. *"Not really,"* he replied, *"but when she was in the river and I was patching her up, something did happen that unnerved me some. It was mid-January, 1983, and I was welding in the engine room one night. I was all alone, and there wasn't another person around for some hundred yards. I shut off my torch and there was silence, except for some talking down below at the bow. I walked forward, thinking some friends of mine had come aboard, but when I got to the bow, the cabin was empty. It struck me awful funny. There was no one else aboard. I went back aft to finish my welding, and when I turned off the torch again, there was that same low-key discussion coming from up front. I listened for awhile, but I couldn't make out what they were saying...I just couldn't understand them. I thought they might be ghosts, and it bothered me for a bit, but I've slept on board since without being molested. She's a well built ship and she's given me a lot of good service. I think Frank Quirk would be proud of her."* Frank's old Gloucester friends, however, prefer not to see the old CAN DO in or around their harbor.

The motley crew of the fishing schooner CLARA SYLVIA, who drowned at Georges Bank but appeared every night on deck. Painting by Trish Cahill.

The hoodoo schooner CHARLES HASKELL of Gloucester. Painting by B. Allen Niff.

Another ship that Gloucester mariners and fishermen banned from their harbor in 1910, was the schooner CLARA SYLVIA. She was the mother-ship for a fleet of five fishing dories. Sailing to Georges Bank from Gloucester with the dories aboard, the CLARA SYLVIA would drop off her fishermen in the dories at the fishing grounds each morning and pick them up before nightfall. This procedure continued each day until the ship was filled with fish. Then, she'd return to port. One morning, the fishermen refused to launch their dories from the CLARA SYLVIA, because they could see that a storm was brewing. The skipper insisted that they go fishing, and since his word was law on the high seas, the ten fishermen obeyed. When the squall hit the Banks, none of the fishermen were able to row their dories back to the mother-ship, and all were lost at sea. Only the skipper and the cook returned to Gloucester in the CLARA SYLVIA. Families of the drowned fishermen, most of them Portuguese, forced the skipper to leave town, fearing for his life. The cook refused to sail again on the CLARA SYLVIA, but the owners found a new skipper, cook, and fishing crew, and the schooner set out again for Georges Bank.

A new fisherman, Mike Randazo, reported, *"once we were at the Banks, each night we'd hear the old crew below cutting up the bait for their trawls, but when we went below to look, there'd be nobody there....The old Portuguese use to sit on the rail at night after fishing and smoke their cigarettes, and at night, we saw them sitting there, smoking."* When the CLARA SYLVIA returned to Gloucester, the new crew of fishermen refused to sail in her again. A third crew was hired, and although the CLARA SYLVIA sailed to another fishing ground, the ghostly visitors appeared every night. Upon returning home, this crew also refused to sail again in the haunted schooner. The owners had to sail the CLARA SYLVIA to Nova Scotia to find a willing crew of fisherman. *"But,"* says Randazo, *"the dead Portuguese crew was always there. They were never seen during the day,—always at night, and they'd hear them cutting up bait below, 'til everyone was scared to go down, or to be on deck after dark."* Nobody knows what finally happened to the CLARA SYLVIA, but she never returned to Gloucester.

The most notorious of Gloucester's hoodoo ships is the CHARLES HASKELL, a fishing schooner, built at Essex, Massachusetts in 1869. Her reputation preceded her into Gloucester Harbor. There, an inspector at Story Shipyard slipped while climbing down her companionway before launching and broke his neck. When the inspector was found dead at the foot of the companionway next morning only a few days before Christmas, the skipper assigned to sail the HASKELL to Georges Bank the day after Christmas refused to go. Clifford Curtis of Gloucester was hired on as captain at the last moment to replace the old superstitious skipper, who announced to the owners that their schooner was cursed.

With a crew of twelve, the HASKELL was at the fishing grounds in February. Having an exceptionally fine day of handlining for cod on March 7th, Captain Curtis was about ready to head back to port with a full load. *"There were over one hundred vessels fishing there that day, forty miles off Georges' North Shoal,"* reported crewman George Scott, but by midafternoon the wind shifted to east-northeast. A storm was brewing and Captain Curtis ordered all the fishermen to haul in their lines and set the storm anchor. By nightfall, the New England fishing fleet was feeling the brunt of a full-fledged hurricane. Other schooners began dragging their anchors and crashing into each other. Captain Curtis himself stood poised over the HASKELL's anchor-cable with an axe, ready to chop the schooner free from her anchor if another boat drifted too near.

The HASKELL strained at her anchor-bit like a bucking bronco for almost six hours. The anchor held tight. Just after midnight, however, crewman George Winters spotted the lanterns aboard another ship bearing down on them at full speed over the rolling waves. Fearing collision, Captain Curtis let the axe fly, cutting the cable, and the HASKELL was adrift, at the mercy of wind and wild sea. The other ship sailed by them, *"'missing us by ten feet,"* reported George Scott. *"We hauled up the foresail and ran for a half an hour. The Captain was worried that we could run aground on North Shoal."*

It wasn't North Shoal, but another ship that the HASKELL smashed into. *"We cut her down abaft of the port rigging,"* said crewman Joe Enos, *"cutting her to the mainmast."* For a moment, the HASKELL was almost sitting on the other vessel. *"One or two or her crew could have jumped aboard us,"* reported Enos, *"but none of them moved. They were shocked. In an instant, their vessel vanished."* The HASKELL's starboard rigging was carried away and the bowsprit was broken. *"We didn't think we'd stay afloat,"* said Enos, *"but then George Winters who was below, shouted up that she was dry. We couldn't believe it."* No vessel had ever survived such a collision without at least springing a leak in her hull, yet the HASKELL was remarkably unscathed. Successfully sailing out the hurricane, she returned to port to report a miraculous recovery and the sinking of the other unknown ship. Two other Gloucester fishing schooners, the PRICE and the MARTHA PORTER, had been lost at Georges Bank during the storm. The vessel the HASKELL accidently sank was the ANDREW JOHNSON out of Salem, with ten men aboard.

Eight members of the HASKELL crew refused to sail on her again.

But Joe Enos, George Winters and George Scott were part of the new crew that joined Captain Curtis aboard the HASKELL at Georges Bank two weeks later. On the sixth day at the fishing grounds, a new man, Harry Richardson, and Joe Enos had the night deck-watch. *"Just after midnight,"* Enos reports, *"Harry grabbed me and pointed to the bow. We saw a group of men in oilskins, dripping wet, standing there. 'They ain't our boys,' said Harry. Then we saw more appear, climbing over the rail from the starboard side. They were like shadows, the shape of men. 'Go wake the skipper,' I told Harry, but he didn't move. 'They're coming aft,' he said, and sure enough, they began stationing themselves along the deck, baiting hooks, and paying no attention to us. We retreated to the wheel-hole and swore to each other that we'd keep quiet about what we were seeing."*

When Joe and Harry were relieved of their watch at two A.M. by George Scott, and a new man named O'Neill, they said nothing of their haunted experience. *"But I was just in my bunk,"* says Joe Enos, *"when I heard a scream, and Scotty shouting, 'All hands on deck!' We all gathered at the companionway and watched the dead-men tending their fishinglines on deck."* O'Neill and Scott were shaking. *"Do you see them?"* Scott kept asking the others over and over again in a loud whisper. *"I see them,"* Captain Curtis finally replied, *"but there's no blood on our hands."* The HASKELL crew then demanded Captain Curtis return to Gloucester and not spend another night on the Banks. They got underway late next day, and next evening after midnight, as they sailed for home, the ten ghosts in oilskins climbed back onto the deck and took up positions along the rails, as if they were fishing. Captain Curtis was at the helm, and one of the ghosts turned to face him, shook its head and smiled.

"As we approached Gloucester Harbor," Joe Enos said, *"the fishermen left our ship and marched over the water towards Salem."* Once the HASKELL arrived back in port, only the captain and Joe Enos agreed to sail in her again. *"Next time we'll bring those fellas back to Salem, before we come into Gloucester,"* said Joe Enos.

The *Salem Gazette* of April 5, 1870, made the public aware of what was happening aboard this spooky ship: *"The CHARLES HASKELL of Gloucester, during her last three voyages is troubled with ghosts....that so frightened the crews of that vessel that they refuse to serve. When she returned from the Banks, spirits appear at times on board and while returning from the last trip they endeavored to induce the Captain to run into Salem, but upon his refusal, they all jumped overboard and disappeared off Eastern Point, Cape Ann. The CHARLES HASKELL is now lying in Gloucester harbor where there is so much excitement with regard to the matter that no crew can be obtained to meet the ghosts again."*

The CHARLES HASKELL never went fishing at Georges Bank again. Her disheartened owners sold her to Dave Hayden of Port Wade, Nova Scotia, where she sailed out of Digby for years, carrying cargoes of wood. The ghosts, to my knowledge, were never seen again, except for one time by Captain Ammon Zinck of Lunenburg, Nova Scotia. He never went into any detail about what he saw and just reported, *"I saw the ghosts on the HASKELL."* There was a popular song about the HASKELL ghosts that was sung along the New England and Nova Scotia coasts well into the 20th century. Part of the old song went as follows:

"....Right over the rail they clambered, all silent one by one,
A dozen dripping sailors, just wait till I am done,
Their faces were pale and sea wan,
Shone through the ghostly night.
Each fellow took his station, as if he had a right.
They moved about before us till land was most in sight,
Or rather I should say so, the lighthouse shone its light.
And then those ghostly sailors moved to the rail again,
And vanished in an instant, before the sons of men."

If the CHARLES HASKELL isn't enough to shiver your timbers, then let's move up the coast a-piece to Maine. The ISADORE, a 400-ton bark, was launched in Kennybunk, about forty years before the HASKELL hit the ways at Essex. She didn't cause a death or injury before or during her launching, but she almost capsized when she hit the water. It was enough to start old time sailors whispering to each other that it was a sign she would be *"a poor sailor; a dangerous vessel to ship-out on."* Crewman Thomas King hadn't heard these unfounded warnings from the old salts until he had already signed aboard for the ISADORE's maiden voyage to New Orleans. He had also received a month's wages in advance from Captain Foss, so his wife could survive while he was away. Some of the other crewmen were having second thoughts as well. Tom King started having nightmares about the upcoming voyage. In his feverish dream, he saw *"seven black coffins, all laid out, side by side at the Kennybunk Wharf."* Jack Haley reported he was having nightmares about the trip too. Two nights before the ISADORE was to depart, Tom King had a vivid nightmare of the coffins on the wharf, but this time he could read the names on each one. They were names of ISADORE crewmen, and he heard a voice distinctly tell him, *"One of these is for you!"*

The morning that the ISADORE made ready to leave port, Tom King walked into Leander Foss's office, returned the advance wages he had received, and told him that he wasn't going to sail. *"It's too late,"* shouted Captain Foss. *"I have not time to replace you, and I'm short-handed as it is. You will either get aboard, or I'll see to it that you go directly to jail— You've signed the contract, and you'll sail with us on the next tide."* Frightened and confused, King left the office and headed for the ship. Crewman Jack Haley arrived at the wharf too late. The ISADORE was already setting sail. But the townsfolk who had gathered at wharfside to watch the ship leave, found a fisherman who was willing to sail Haley out to the ISADORE so he wouldn't miss the voyage. One bystander heard Haley say, as he threw his bag into the sailboat, *"I wish I had missed her!"*

The ISADORE was but out of sight when a sudden snow-squall lashed the Maine coast. Next morning, the wreckage of the Kennybunk bark was washed ashore at Bald Hill Cliff, Ogunquit, as were seven bodies from the ISADORE, including Jack Haley's. The others sank beneath the raging surf under a 90 foot high precipice of rock known as "The Pulpit." There were no survivors. Kennybunk went into mourning. The old salts had been right about her, and Thomas King's fateful dreams should have been heeded. Mrs. King was devastated, she felt that she had forced her husband to take the voyage. Two days later, however, she was elated, for who came walking in the front door, wet and exhausted? None other than her husband, Thomas King! *"But they said no one survived the wreck,"* she screamed, hugging the trembling man. *"How did you escape?"* "I didn't," Tom replied. And he was as shocked as she, for Tom hadn't heard that the ISADORE had wrecked. When he left Captain Foss' office, he didn't go to the ship. Instead, he ran into the woods, and had been hiding out there, through the storm, for two days. He was ashamed and felt a coward, but was so hungry that he had decided to sneak home, even though he thought his wife would scold him. Surprisingly, no one in town ridiculed Tom King for his actions. *"He had only heeded God's warning, which was right,"* they concluded. Tom King did, however, feel guilty, and he soon moved away to live the remainder of his life in Holliston, Massachusetts.

Tom King's experience makes one wonder if these stories of spooky ships are but the fears and fables of superstitious sailors and seaside dwellers or, are in fact, the forces of powers beyond human understanding. As I sit here writing, with the black-hulled GRAMPUS bobbing at her mooring outside my door, I understand the deep brooding of those superstitious old salts of bygone days. Still, superstitions don't explain why so many sailors saw the ghosts aboard the CLARA SYLVIA and the CHARLES HASKELL, or why Jack Haley and Tom King had premonitions about the sinking of the ISADORE.

II
Visiting Our Local Vampires

The boy from Brockton wasn't quite right in the head, but the judge wouldn't let him plead insanity. The judge did, however, accept his plea of *"vampirism."* The boy had killed his grandmother and then started sucking her blood. He had a need to do it, he told the jury. He had been brought up on horse-blood sandwiches and became addicted to drinking blood with every meal. This wasn't a macabre case from the days of Dracula or the Dark Ages, but occurred in 1981 in Brockton, Massachusetts—it wasn't the first time vampirism reared its ugly, bat-like head in New England. In the previous two centuries, there were at least three cases of vampirism or assumed vampirism in Rhode Island—only 25 miles from Brockton—and two more in Vermont.

"A vampire," Webster explains in his dictionary, is a *"blood sucking ghost or reanimated body of a dead person believed to come from the grave and wander about by night sucking the blood of persons asleep. One who lives by preying on others; a blood sucker; commonly a woman who uses her attractions to bring her lover to a debased or impoverished condition. Also a Vampire Bat, any of various bats popularly but erroneously believed to suck the blood of animals..."*

In the early 1770s, a Rhode Island farmer named Stuckley, the father of 14 children, feared that his oldest daughter Sarah was a vampire. Sarah ruled the roost, bossing her other brothers and sisters, and occasionally her mother and father as well. She seemed to take great delight in slaughtering the farm animals. The younger children complained to their parents that Sarah licked the blood from her fingers as if it were honey or jelly. In her early twenties, Sarah suddenly contracted consumption, and within a few months she was dead. Shortly after Sarah was buried, one of her younger sisters began coughing up blood. The local doctor diagnosed her disease as the supposedly incurable consumption, later known as tuberculosis. In her delirium, the younger sister told the parents that the ghost of Sarah visited her each night to sit on her stomach in an attempt to suffocate her and suck blood from her neck. The highly contagious consumption spread through the family, and as five more of the Stuckley children became ill and slowly suffocated to death, they all complained of nightly visits from Sarah. Half of Farmer Stuckley's family was wiped out within two years.

When his wife took ill, and also complained of nightmares in which Sarah came to her, seemingly for destructive purposes, he decided to take action. He, with the help of neighbors, exhumed the body of his daughter,

Sarah. Opening the casket, they found her remarkably well-preserved, her hair and fingernails still growing, which to Stuckley and his friends was enough to suspect that Sarah was a vampire who left her grave each night to suck blood from the living. When they cut into Sarah's body, they discovered that her heart was still filling with blood. This was the damning proof of vampirism. Farmer Stuckley cut his eldest daughter's heart out, placed it in an iron pot in front of his house, and with all the neighbors as witness, burned the heart to a crisp. The ritual over, everyone went home, and two weeks later, Mrs. Stuckley died of consumption.

Exactly 100 years later, 1874, the *Providence Journal* recorded that *"in the Village of Placedale, Rhode Island, William Rose dug up the body of his daughter and burned her heart, for she was drawing energy from other members of the family."* Although the reporter doesn't say that the reason for William Rose's action was fear that his daughter was a vampire, it's obvious that his bizarre ritual was to combat vampirism. *"If the heart of one of the family who dies of consumption is taken and burned out,"* reports Daniel Ransom in his Memoirs of the 19th century, *"others would be free of it."* Daniel's own brother, Frederick Ransom, died of consumption in 1817 in Vermont. *"Father, having some faith in the remedy,"* writes Daniel, *"had the heart of Frederick taken out after he had been buried, and it was burned at Captain Pearson's blacksmith forge. However, it did not prove a remedy, for mother, sister, and two brothers died with that disease afterward."*

In the first week of October, 1890, the *Boston Transcript* reported a story of vampirism at Woodstock, Vermont, where some fifty years earlier, four local doctors of high intelligence and education, burned the heart of a man named Corwin who had died of consumption. The entire population of Woodstock gathered on the Green to witness the burning of the heart in an iron pot. Once the heart had turned to ashes, it, still in the pot, was buried 15 feet down into the center of the Green, and a granite boulder weighing many tons was set on top of it. Then, all was covered up, the blood of a bull sprinkled over, and the Green was reseeded, as if the event had never taken place. This was done to save the vampire Corwin's brother, who was also dying from consumption, obviously caught from his dead brother, who visited each evening to suck the life-blood out of him. When the body of the dead Corwin was exhumed six months after the burial, as expected, Doctor Joseph Gallup discovered that *"the vampire's heart contained its victim's blood."* Thus, the exorcism on the Green was considered a necessary, if gruesome, procedure by Gallup and the three other doctors of the village. Even more ghastly is that the sick Mr. Corwin was to swallow some of the ashes of his dead brother's heart, mixed with bull's blood, in order the break the vampire's curse and reverse the progressive wasting away of the victims body.

The most celebrated case of vampirism occured less than 100 years ago at Wickford and Exeter, Rhode Island. Again, vampirism fears were aroused because of an outbreak of tuberculosis within a family. George Brown's wife Mary of Exeter, died of the disease on December 8, 1883. Within six months, her daughter Mary, age 20, passed away of the same dreaded disease after much suffering. George Brown had six more daughters, and only one son Edwin. Edwin was married and owned his own farm at West Wickford, some five miles away from his parent's home. Five years after his sister Mary died, Edwin contracted tuberculosis, and fearful that he'd die after long suffering like his sister and mother, he moved to the Rocky Mountains to improve his health. There, less than a year later, he received word that his younger sister Mercy Brown, age 19, had also died of tuberculosis. Edwin headed back East in 1892, determined to lick the plaque that was slowly but surely wiping out his whole family.

In Colorado, the popular cure for combating tuberculosis was to *"eat the fried heart of a rattlesnake,"* but Edwin had also learned during his New England upbringing, that vampires were the cause of spreading the disease, and that the burning of the heart of the vampire was the cure. He didn't know which of his deceased family members were causing his blood to be sapped, so he had all three bodies exhumed. His mother and Mary were skeletal, but sister Mercy, dead only two months, looked fresh as the day she was buried. Her heart was examined by the Exeter physician, and *"whole-blood was found in her heart,"* meaning only one thing, *"Mercy was a vampire!"* Right there at the Chestnut Hill Cemetery in Exeter, Mercy's heart was cut out of her body, and the body was reburied. The heart was then burned at the stake nearby, and like all the rattlesnake hearts he had eaten in the Rockies, Edwin chomped on the fried heart of his sister Mercy, with the hope that his sickness would soon go away. The grisly cure didn't work however, and Edwin Brown died a few weeks later.

So you see, Count Dracula and blood-sucking bats are but childish fairytales compared to our robust New England vampires—Eat your hearts out you Transylvanian wimps!

III
Never Catch Old Sasquatch

Sasquatch, Yeti, the Abominable Snowman, Bigfoot, or whatever you want to call it, doesn't seem to be as popular in New England as it is in Washington, Oregon, Western Canada, and the Tibetan mountains. This illusive monster gets a lot of publicity in the Northwest region of our country, but little here, yet sightings of Sasquatch are fairly common, and have been since before the coming of the White Man to these shores. The Indian tribes had various names for this tall, robust hairy creature, but through the centuries, most anthropologists thought that it was a mythical animal, or a disfigured bear that hunting parties would encounter from time to time and report as a monster of exaggerated height and bulk. It was the Indians who gave it the name *"Sasquatch,"* on the West Coast, and a similar creature was called *"Wendigo,"* here on the East Coast. Basically, both mean *"Outcast."* A report from a remote Hudson Bay Company outpost at Lake of the Clouds, Canada, in 1774, mentions that local Indians had captured a strange *"large animal that resembled man and walked on two feet, but had no neck and was covered with fur."* But there were no further reports on this Yeti-like creature from the Hudson Bay representatives.

In and around Topsfield, Maine near the Canadian border, a seven foot Sasquatch, who the locals call *"Indian Devil,"* is spotted periodically, and is an offshoot of Penobscot mythology. This mammoth creature with reddish brown hair and facial features of a human being, has always been part of Maine Indian lore. The oversized creature is supposedly kind and gentle, but a killer if aroused or bothered in any way. At Maine's highest mountain, Katahdin, where Indians believed all storms originated, the Indian Devil called *"Pomoola,"* half man-half beast, reigned over the countryside. In 1866, the first White Man to see *"Pomoola,"* was a miner and mountain climber named Mike Cluey. *"It was a manlike creature covered with red hair,"* he reported. *"It was on the opposite bank of a pond, eating live, raw fish. It was there at Twilight and again at Dawn, but it didn't see me."* Cluey described it as being about seven feet tall, and his Indian friends said that Pomoola would kill animals and even Indians, but would not kill White Men, but they didn't know why it discriminated. Possibly, it just didn't like white meat. The hot-headed, red-haired giant of Mount Katahdin had been seen as recently as September 15th, 1988, by a group of mountain climbing boy scouts from Massachusetts, and by six out of state campers, who described it as having a *"tan triangular face, reddish brown fur, and extremely broad shoulders."* It was grubbing for roots near the edge of the forest, about half way up the mountain, when they saw it from a distance. *"It made fright-*

ening sounds," said one boy scout. *"It stunk like rotten eggs,"* reported another of the frightened boys. The strange sulphuric odor lingered in the area for hours after the Sasquatch retreated back into the forest.

It is difficult for many people to believe that Bigfoot creatures exist, let alone one that has been Indian legend for thousands of years, and especially one that has bright red hair. But over 100 years ago, a similar creature was encountered on the Vermont-Massachusetts border near Williamstown. It made headlines in the *New York Times*: *"Wildman Of The Mountains Scares Two Young Vermont Hunters."* The young men described the creature they ran into as *"resembling a man in form and movement, but covered all over with bright red hair, and having a long straggling beard, and with very wild eyes.... When first seen, the creature sprang from behind a rocky cliff, and started for the woods nearby, when, mistaking it for a bear, one of the men fired, and, it is thought, wounded it, for with fierce cries of pain and rage, it turned on its assailants, drawing them before it at high speed. They lost their guns and ammunition in their flight and dared not return for fear of encountering the strange being."*

Although there have not been any recent sightings of the red-headed Sasquatch at Williamstown, an occasional anguished desperate cry echoes through the mountains of nearby Pownal, Vermont. It is thought to be that of a Bigfoot creature. *"The cry and its smell are distinctive,"* says Yeti-expert Peter Byrne of Ireland's Wicklow Mountains. Mr. Byrne has spent his life tracking down Bigfoot in America and Canada. *"The unearthly screech of a Bigfoot,"* he says, *"cannot be confused with that of any other creature."* The bone-chilling screech has been heard in the mountainous woodlands near Rutland, Vermont as well, and there have been some recent sightings there, of what is described as an eight-foot Yeti, *"black colored with white chest markings."* It was first spotted in May of 1974, digging for roots in a pasture, by a Rutland farmer and his family; and in the same field in 1986, by a young married couple; and the following year by a local man named John Miller, at about Dusk, only a mile from the earlier sightings. Miller described it as *"a black gorilla-like animal that looked almost ten feet tall."* Skeptics might take solace in the fact that the gorilla, whose existence we accept today without a second thought, was considered a creature of fiction and myth until the year 1902, and wasn't accepted as a real animal until the early 1930's.

Another big black hairy beast has been spotted near Mount Israel and Sandwich Dome, New Hampshire, off and on, since about 1942. Footprints, three feet long and eight inches wide, of a heavy four-toed creature were recently discovered embedded in the mud just off the Highway at Sandwich. The Sasquatch, unlike the bear, has four toes rather than five, and does not have claws, therefore it is assumed that the prints were those of an unknown creature weighing over 500 pounds.

Doctor John Napier, curator at Smithsonian Institution, suggests that Bigfoot may be the missing-link of humanity, and an offshoot of our Neanderthal ancestors. *"There has been a tremendous revival of public interest in Bigfoot within the last twenty years,"* says Napier, *"and like New Hampshire's Peyton Place, what we know of early written records here, the story of Sasquatch has been continuing for a great many years."* At New Hampshire's Squam Mountain, while driving the mountain road one recent evening, John Oswald and his family were surprised and petrified when a Sasquatch *"leaped into our headlights. It was a furry creature seven feet tall,"* he reported to the New Hampshire State Police. *"It was strong looking, with big shoulders and a big nose. It's face was triangular shaped,"* he said, *"but once it saw us in the car, it backed away and bolted into the woods."*

Probably the most well known Bigfoot encounter in New England, was one experienced by Gerald St. Louis and two boys at a parking lot in Hollis, New Hampshire, near the Massachusetts line. It was on the night of May 7, 1977, that Gerald, with two twelve-year old boys who were to assist him at a flea-market in the morning, decided to camp overnight in his truck at the lot and be up bright and early to open the market in the morning. They were parked flanking the nearby woods, with no other vehicle, building, or human being in sight of them. *"At about ten o'clock that night,"* Gerald reported, *"I opened the truck door and started to step outside, when I saw it face to face. It was all hairy, brown colored, and eight or nine feet tall, with long arms and long hair. Thank God for the lights that came on when I opened the door, for they startled the creature and it ran toward a fence about four and a half feet high, and it jumped over it with ease. I could see it standing there in the distance, just looking at us. I drove out of there so fast,"* Gerald concluded, *"that I left everything I was going to sell the next day behind on the ground."*

Two other flea-market sellers, Stan Evans and Jeff Warren, who were parked in a truck some 300 yards away from Gerald and the boys, also got a scare from apparently the same Bigfoot. Their truck was shaken like a ragdoll by *"some hairy animal,"* as they called it, which frightened them enough to leave the scene as well, although they weren't aware until days later of what had happened to Gerald. Bigfoot tracks measuring almost 17 inches long and 7 inches wide were found on the morning after both incidents.

"People around here have reported seeing Bigfoot tracks and even Bigfoot creatures themselves for the past ten years," said Marianne Cascio of Agawam, Massachusetts in a recent interview. Throughout the 1970's and

1980's there were numerous police reports of townsfolk encountering *"a hairy wild man over seven-feet tall,"* along the dirt roads near the outskirts of Agawam, near the Connecticut border. When Bigfoot tracks were discovered in the soft dirt and snow on the banks of the Westfield River, near Robinson State Park, George Earley, a former U.S. aerospace administrator and Bigfoot buff, went to the park to study the big footprints. They measured 27 1/2 inches by 8 inches, and Earley thought they were made by a Sasquatch, but couldn't be sure. They were so deeply embedded however, that Earley judged the weight of the beast to be over 700 lbs.

Some twenty miles away, the first recorded Connecticut encounter with Sasquatch occurred in August, 1895 at Colebrook. The *Hartford Courant* reports that Selectman Riley W. Smith and his pet bulldog were attacked by a wild man while they were in a field picking blueberries. *"While I was stooping over picking berries,"* says Selectman Smith, *"my bulldog, noted for its pluck, ran with a whine to me and stationed itself between my legs. A second afterwards, a large man, stark naked, and covered with hair all over his body, ran out of a clump of bushes, and with fearful yells and cries, made for the woods at lightning speed, where he soon disappeared....I admit that I was badly scared and that my dog was fairly paralyzed. This all happened at Colebrook near the Lewis place."*

"Hairy men," and other strange creatures have been a constant bother to folks living on the outskirts of the Hockamock Swamp at Bridgewater, Massachusetts. The Indians who lived around the swamp before the White Man came, avoided the Hockamock Swamp after sunset, and feared entering it to hunt or fish even in the daylight. The descriptions of animals said to live in the swamp were extremely farfetched—snakes with three heads, crocodile-like fish, giant ravenous wolf-like birds, and of course, giant hairy men, whose haunting wail from the swamp meant the impending death of a warrior or chief. On April 9, 1970, the *Boston Herald* newspaper reported that *"a thing, all hairy, has been seen by many people at Bridgewater,"* and, *"large footprints have been found in the mud, thought to be left behind by a seven foot bear."* Bridgewater Police and Massachusetts State Police with attack dogs, were called out to search around the swamp, which they did for two days and nights, and the calls kept coming in from people who were seeing a large bear-like creature, standing upright, but sometimes running off on all fours. Yet, there hadn't been a bear in the area for over 100 years, or more. Also, two local policemen sitting in their cruiser on the night of April 8th, reported sheepishly that, *"without warning, something began to pick up the rear of our car. I spun the car around and got my spotlight on something that looked like a bear running around the corner of a nearby house."* When the policeman was asked if the creature could have been a

Sasquatch, he shrugged his shoulders, looked embarrased and walked away. The police could accept being frightened by an illusive bear, but not by the legendary Bigfoot of Hockamock Swamp. Reports of sighting of the bear-like creature have died down since then in the town of Bridgewater, but now and again the local police get a call that some strange hairy beast is seen coming or going in or out of the swamp or creeping along its fringes.

A similar *"ape man"* was recently reported walking along the Brunswick Road to Durham, Maine, in broad daylight, by four motorists. Neota Huntington of Durham told a reporter of the *Portland Press Herald* that the 400 lb. hairy creature frightened her three children to such an extent that her twelve year old daughter Lois fell off her bike and skinned her knee badly. *"It just stood there and looked at me laying there on the ground,"* Lois said later. *"It was an ape-man with shaggy black fur,"* said Mrs. Huntington. *"It stood there by the side of the road, just looking down at Lois and at the other two, ages ten and eight, who were paralyzed with fear, and then it wandered off into the woods. I called the police, but nobody seemed to believe me or the kids."*

Two teenaged girls of Manchester, Maine, also reported the sighting of a Sasquatch on the Old Camp Road, just outside Maine's capital city of Augusta. This ape-man was seven feet tall, *"with brown fur, and markings of white on its chest and stomach."* The girls came upon it from behind, and at first it didn't see them. It was on the side of the road, hiding behind a tree, watching a farmer cutting wood. *"The creature was swaying back and forth,"* said one of the girls, which apparently is a trait of Sasquatches. *"It was some twenty yards from us, and quite a distance from the man cutting wood, but seeing it, my friend Mary screamed. It turned to face us. It looked like an ape's face only tan. Mary kept screaming, which seemed to frighten the creature. It, at first, didn't seem to know which way to go, but then it crossed the road and ran into the woods."* The police were called out to search for the creature, but they had no success, and the farmer cutting wood said that he heard the girls screaming, but didn't see the Sasquatch. Six week later, however, at approximately the same location on the Old Camp Road, a woman sitting in a parked car waiting for her husband to come out of a nearby house, saw this same *"ape-like"* creature, *"standing by a tree, swaying."* She sounded her horn, which startled the creature, and it reacted in confusion as it did when the girls screamed. Then, it started running towards the car, which unsettled the woman, so she blew the horn again. Her husband, thinking his wife was getting impatient, came out of the house, and caught just a glimpse of the Sasquatch running into the woods. The woman, who wishes to remain anonymous to avoid ridicule, said that the sound of the horn the second time frightened the ape-man away. It was, she said, *"the most frightening experience of my life."*

One can understand the overwhelming fear of coming face-to-face with a Sasquatch, or even seeing this monster at a distance, but what bothers many is that hunters who live in areas where Bigfoot has been spotted, threaten to shoot it, if for no other reason than to prove it exists. To shoot one would be a shame, possibly even murder, for the creature may be partly human— or the "missing link," as many anthropologists are hoping. After all, those who have met up with it say it stinks terribly and makes bone-chilling noises. Don't we have enough creatures like that in our society today? Let's allow old Sasquatch to remain an evasive mystery and we'll all be better off.

The Demon of Dover

IV
The Delicate Demon of Dover

I talked to the police chief of Dover, Carl Sheridan. He had been police chief twelve years earlier, too, when it all happened. Being an old law enforcement man myself, I was sure that the chief would be straight with me. *"Did it really happen, or was it a hoax of some sort?"* I asked him. *"It was real,"* he replied. *"Those boys really did see something out there."*

"Has anything like it happened around Dover since then? Has the creature been seen again within the last twelve years?"

"Not to my knowledge," replied the Chief, *"but it sure caused a stir to this little place back then, and people around here still talk about it. It was weird, really weird."*

Bill Bartlett, Mike Mazzocca and Andy Brodie were teenagers then. It was April, and Spring was in the night air. They were just riding around in Bill's Volkswagen, gabbing about girls and potential Summer jobs. Farm Street is narrow and winding, flanked by woods and pastures. As the car poked along, heading towards Smith Street, something loomed up in the headlights. *"At first I thought it was an animal, frozen or stunned by the headlights,"* said Bill. *"But then I realized that I was looking at some unusual human-like creature. It was climbing over a stone wall, creeping along near the road. It looked to be less than four-feet tall, with a large head shaped like an egg, but it was as big as the biggest of watermelons. It had round glassy eyes that kept staring at the headlights. It didn't move for almost a minute, so I got a good look at it. The eyes were red and its skin, peach colored, almost like a baby's, and it had no hair that I could see. It didn't seem to have any nose or mouth or ears, but a thin neck that didn't seem strong enough to suport the large head. It had long spindly legs and arms with big hands and fingers. It seemed to be clutching at the rocks with its fingers and toes....I must confess,"* said Bill, *"at seeing it, I panicked, screamed and sped off down the road. We returned later that night with others to that same spot, but the creature, soon to be called 'The Dover Demon,' was not to be seen by us again that night."*

Interviewing Bill Bartlett twelve years later, in January, 1989, now age 29; his story hadn't changed. *"The creature had a bloated look,"* he recalled, *"and was almost weak looking, like one of those malnutritioned kids you often see on television....It had a featureless expression, almost sad, like it was starving."*

Two hours after Bill, Mike, and Andy had their encounter, John Baxter, age 16, was walking home from his girlfriend's house on Millers' Hill Road, not far from Farm Street. John was hoping to thumb a ride home, but he saw no cars on the road, so he started trudging the road slowly into the night. Coming the other way, walking up the street on the opposite side off the road, was a little dark figure, which John assumed was an acquaintance of his named Mat Bouchard, who lived near his girlfriend's house. It was almost midnight, but John didn't think it was too unusual to see the young Bouchard boy out walking near his own home. *"Hey Bouchard, how are ya?"* he shouted across the road as they were about to pass. But he didn't get a response. Then he realized that the little figure standing some twenty feet away was not Bouchard. It stopped, as did John. *"Who is that?"* he shouted. It was the same creature Bill Bartlett had seen earlier that evening. *"It was a little over three feet tall,"* John described it, *"and it looked like a big monkey with a large figure-eight head....Like a big baby with long arms and legs....It just stood there staring at me, and I started shaking in my boots. When you see something like that, you don't want to stick around to see what it's going to do. I was hypnotized, and I really thought it was going to jump at me, but it just stared for what seemed like ten minutes. It was clutching at rocks and little trees by the roadside, as if for support, keeping its big, shiny, orange eyes on me. Then, as quick as a wink, it turned and scurried down the road and over a hill into the woods. I turned and raced away, flagging down a car when I got to the intersection of Farm Street, and I got a ride all the way home."*

Neither Bill Bartlett nor John Baxter had heard of the other's experience until later the next day. They met later and shared stories of their encounters. Neither boy knew the other prior to their mutual experience, yet their descriptions of the creature matched perfectly. Two nights later, Bill Taintor of Devon, and Abby Brabham of Sherborn, also saw the Demon at night by the side of Springdale Avenue, near downtown Dover. As with Bill Bartlett, the creature seemed attracted to Taintor's car headlights. Bill and Abby, who were deeply shaken by the experience, described it as *"beige colored with a big oblong head, no nose and no tail, with big eyes that glowed green in the headlights."* Neither the police, parents, nor friends of those who saw the creature doubted their stories, and even after all the years that have passed since those April nights in 1977, the eye-witnesses stick to their stories. It was not a teenage prank or hoax.

Many so-called experts, including Walter Webb, a Director of Boston's Museum of Science, investigated the sightings of this little gnome-like creature called the Dover Demon, and were satisfied that it does exist. Newspaper reporters flooded the little village of Dover, population 5,000, got their story and left, and the incidents were soon forgotten, except, of course, by those who live in Dover. Although only fifteen miles from metropolitan Boston, Dover is deep in the woods, off the beaten track, and except for their Demon, it is usually undisturbed. Why, one wonders, did this delicate, peach-skinned, nocturnal creature choose quiet little Dover as its nesting place? We shall probably never know. An evening drive down Farm Street, or a stroll to the corner store for milk or bread, or even a quiet bicycle ride at Dusk in Dover, never fails to bring a chill to the nape of one's neck. For who knows when the shy little Demon of Dover might decide to show its ugly head again.

The Boogeyman of Beggerly.

V
Boogeyman Of Beggerly

The first person to petition an American court to change the name of something—namely a village— was Roger Conant, the founder of Gloucester, Salem and Beverly, Massachusetts. Conant and his fishermen had been forced out of Gloucester by Miles Standish, the Pilgrim's military leader, and two years later, in 1629, they were evicted from Salem by Governor Endicott, the Puritan leader. Four fishermen and their families, namely Conant, John Balch, Peter Palfrey and John Woodbury, were given 200 acres across the river from their Salem homes by Endicott, who didn't want their fishy business or their growing of *"that filthy weed"* tobacco in his new, pure town of Salem. Conant's new settlement was called Beverly but the Salem Puritans across the river called it *"Beggerly!"*

The fishermen didn't take kindly to the name bestowed upon their new settlement, so Conant petitioned the General Court, stood before the magistrates and said, *"a great dislike and discontent of our people for this name, Beverly, is upon us, because we are a small place. It has caused on us a nickname of Beggerly, and we request that the name of our small settlement be changed."* Conant's request was denied. The name Beverly and the nickname Beggerly have remained to this day. The nickname is usually not used by Salemites except during the annual Thanksgiving Day football rivalry, when the Beverly Panthers take on the Salem Witches.

Throughout the centuries, notoriety visited Salem especially in the seventeenth century, as the center for witch hysteria; and in the eighteenth, although Beverly became the *"Birthplace of the American Navy,"* Salem stole Beverly's thunder by producing the greatest fleet of privateersmen, and the most successful bevy of legal pirates in America. Even today, in fame and popularity, Salem far exceeds neighbor Beverly, and Beverly must be content to live in the shadow of the Witch City. Like Salem, however, Beggerly has its fair share of witches, ghosts, goblins, and things that go bump in the night. Probably the most underrated beastly character of the dark underworld is the Boogeyman, a deliciously chilling fellow from our childhood days—but fear not, he is alive and well in Beggerly, and was recently encountered by a good friend of mine.

Steve Barsanti, now a young, handsome veterinarian, moved to Beverly from Lynnfield as a teenager. He, with his parents, two brothers and a sister moved into a 32-room mansion on Woodbury Street, overlooking Beverly Harbor. The street coincidentally was named for one of the four founders of the town, John Woodbury. The house had been built about the turn of the century for the Czechoslovakian Ambassador. Beggerly lost its poor hand-me-down image in the 1800's when it became a popular summer resort for America's rich and powerful. *"The house had been unoccupied for a number of years before my father purchased it in 1965,"* said Steve, *"and I remember the real-estate lady telling us that the large ornate living room on the first floor had been used many times to wake corpses of past residents who had died in the house. The spacious, shadowy kitchen with three pantries, was, at first, my mother's favorite room, but soon, she confided to me and my older brother, she constantly felt the presence of someone unseen in the kitchen. My brother and I felt it too, like someone was watching us. I often found myself staring into one of the three pantries expecting to see someone appear, and a hollow feeling enveloped me whenever I entered the kitchen. There were times in the evening when I wanted a snack from the kitchen, but I would have to walk down a narrow back stairway to get there. Not only was I always reluctant to do so, but my dog absolutely refused to take the stairway that led from my third floor bedroom to the kitchen. If I decided to brave the stairway alone, she would sit at the head of the stairs, her head bent to watch me tiptoe around the corner, and she would groan and wail until I returned."*

Almost every morning since the day they moved in, Mr. Barsanti found the kitchen door that led to the backyard open. He would scold the children, but all four strongly denied leaving the door open. Steve's mother insisted that burglars were coming in at night, disrupting the pantries, which she found in disaray almost every morning, and moving the kitchen table, which she discovered in a different part of the kitchen almost every morning. Frightened, the Barsantis had new locks made for all the downstairs doors, including the kitchen door leading to the outside, which Mr. Barsanti had double-locked on the inside and outside. *"My father figured that, if he locked the doors himself at night before he went to bed,"* explained Steve, *"these strange occurrences would stop—but they didn't. They, in fact, seemed to increase, baffling my mother, frustrating my father, and I have to admit, titillating my brothers, sister, and I."*

"I do have to admit, however, that finding a double-locked kitchen door open in the morning, did send shivers up and down my spine. And whenever I felt obliged to enter the kitchen at night, alone, I moved along about my business as quickly as possible, never looking left or right into one of those pantries, always feeling that someone was at my heels, ready to pounce on me."

Two years after they moved in, Mrs. Barsanti and Steve had a strange disturbing experience when they were alone in the house one rainy afternoon.

She was in the front hall at the foot of a 32-foot high spiral staircase that led to the second and third floors. It was a beautiful, wide flowing stairway carpeted in royal red, with white wood paneling and an open view to all floors including the doors of all rooms on the upper floors. Mrs. Barsanti saw someone enter her husband's office on the second floor. Thinking it was Steve, she shouted, *"Steve, stay out of your father's office."* Steve was in another room on the first floor, and hearing his mother yell at him, he stepped into the front hall. She was so dumbfounded that, at first, she couldn't speak. Then she shouted that there was an intruder on the second floor. *"My first impulse was to run to the phone and call for the police,"* said Steve, then aged 18. *"But as I did so, my mother and I both saw a figure leap from the balcony located outside my father's second story office."* Neither Steve nor his mother saw or heard the intruder hit the ground—all they saw was a dark figure leap into the air and fall. *"Even at the time,"* said Steve, *"I questioned whether or not it was a human being."* The police were called and Mr. Barsanti, who had been away on business returned, but nothing in his office, nor in the rest of the house, had been taken or disturbed.

"After that episode," says Steve, *"I kept a loaded World War II German nine-milimeter pistol on the nightstand beside my bed. It was my father's, retrieved from an unfortunate soldier during the war. Both my father and I had great respect for that pistol, so to protect it, I placed a piece of rabbit fur over the nightstand and placed the lamp, alarm clock and then the gun on the fur piece."*

For most of the following summer, Steve was left alone in the house. The rest of the family had gone off to vacation at their lakeside cottage in New Hampshire. Steve was a lifeguard in Beverly and had to remain behind. One evening, returning home after being out with his pals until about midnight, he settled into bed on the third floor and fell asleep, his gun on the table beside him. He was rudely awakened by a hideous laugh at three A.M. It was an evil echoing laugh coming from someone standing at the foot of his bed, but it was so dark, Steve couldn't see a thing. *"I was paralyzed with fear,"* said Steve, *"my ears bursting with this loud hideous laugh, my eyes bulging, yet I was unable to see the intruder. Shaking off the initial shock, I quickly rolled out of bed and onto the narrow corridor between my bed and the wall of my room, groping for the pistol on the nighttable as I hit the floor. I couldn't find the gun at first. There was something different about the table. It was as if the lamp, clock and gun had been rearranged, and the rabbit fur was gone, or at least missing from the nightstand. My fingers felt the cold steel of the pistol and I hugged it to my chest, but the shock of my table being rearranged by some unseen hand, heightened my fear, if that was possible at this time, for I was all but frozen to the floor. Gasping for breath, I listened. The laughing had stopped, but I thought I heard heavy breathing from across my little room. Was it a burglar, or a prankster, or a family member returned home and trying to frighten me. I dared not fire my pistol on the slight chance it was a mischievous friend or brother. I laid on the floor for a full fifteen minutes, yet it seemed like an eternity. I tried to locate and distinguish every sound I heard from the creaking old house. I concluded that it had to be a brazen intruder who knew enough not to move, waiting patiently for me to make the first move so he could perhaps frighten me into a corner."*

Steve finally built up enough courage to shout at the interloper. *"I've got a loaded gun,"* he said, *"and I'm not afraid to use it."* He waited for a response, thinking that the man would either attempt escape, or come rushing at him. Neither happened. There was no response, no noise. *"Whoever you are, either identify yourself, or leave this house immediately....I will not harm you or try to stop you."* Steve waited again for a response, but there was none. Feeling cramped and vulnerable, Steve moved to a sitting position on the floor beside the bed, keeping the gun pointed in front of him, fingers of both hands on the trigger. *"I am crazy on living,"* Steve shouted, almost hysterically this time. *"Any further attempt to frighten me or approach me, will be met with a burst from my semi-automatic nine-milimeter pistol."* Listening to his own heavy breathing, minutes passed. *"I finally decided,"* said Steve, *"that the only reasonable course of action was for me to leave the house, but it took me awhile to decide whether I would take the front stairway, which was open to all those doors that people could pop out of, or the narrow winding back stairway that led to the kitchen. When I decided, I yelled out my plan to the intruder—'I am going to leave the house by the back stairway. If you interfere, you will be met with a pitiless burst from my semi-automatic nine-milimeter pistol. If you think I will encounter you on the way, you should speak up now.' "* Steve listened, but there was no response to his escape plan.

Slowly and as quietly as possible, he lifted himself from the floor, and with one hand probing the darkness before him, and the other ready to squeeze the trigger of the pistol, he moved slowly forward in a crouched position. Tiptoeing from the bed to the bureau, he found the keys to the kitchen door and his car, stuffed them into the elastic band of his jockey-underwear and moved on towards the back stairway. *"I had to pass the bathroom and two bedrooms before I came to the light switch that illuminated the back staircase, but by the time I got to the second floor, the light I turned on was obscured, so I grabbed for the light-chain on the second floor landing. There was a bright flash and then the bulb frizzled out. Now I knew I was dealing with more than a human intruder. I dashed down the stairs, my body and spirit flooded with panic. Landing with a thud in the kitchen, I suddenly realized I was standing in the spookiest room in the house. I would have to pass the three pantries, where knives and other chopping weapons were stored, and then would have to put down the gun to properly set the keys in the locks to open the back door. I have never felt such fear and suffocation. Instead of the intruder trapping me, I had trapped myself."*

Steve tiptoed across the creaking kitchen floor, chills creeping down his spine as he passed the three seemingly possessed pantries. He easily slipped one lock, then fumbling with the keys, his hands shaking terribly, he managed to unlock the back door. *"I went bounding out into the night,"* said Steve, *"sucking in deep gulps of fresh air."* His car was parked under a covered car-port near the kitchen. *"But even after I jumped into the car,"* he said, *"I was still fearful. As I backed out of the driveway, I thought I might be attacked from the bushes."*

Now Steve was driving the back roads of Beverly, a loaded pistol on the front seat beside him, dressed in only white jockey shorts. He kept driving from road to road until night turned to Dawn. Realizing that heavy morning commuter traffic would soon commence and that his neighbors would soon be up and around, Steve had to return home. He had no choice. If for nothing more than to put on some clothes. He drove back to the house, slowly up the driveway, examining all the windows of the old house, looking for a light, or a strange face. *"I felt like someone was watching me all this time,"* says Steve. *"I parked as close as I could to the kitchen door, and grabbing the gun I ran back into the house. I found the kitchen door wide open. I, of course, had left it open. Once inside the kitchen, I slowly scanned the room, looking for the intruder. Then I noticed, placed on the kitchen table, folded like a fancy napkin, was the rabbit fur that had been on my bedroom nightstand. I had certainly not brought it into the kitchen, and the only time I had noticed it gone from the nightstand was when I was groping for the gun while the intruder laughed at me."* Steve left the house immediately, closing and locking the kitchen door behind him. He grabbed an old pair of paint pants from the garage and drove barefooted up to New Hampshire to join the rest of his family. From there, he went off to school in the fall.

"My father sold the house a few weeks later," said Steve, *"and since my terrifying encounter, I never returned to that house again. Some might say that I imagined the laughing man at the foot of my bed, or that it was part of a bad dream. But I didn't imagine or dream the rabbit fur folded neatly on the kitchen table—that was real— and as far as I'm concerned, so was that Boogeyman."*

VI
Haunted Islands Of Boston Bay

Islands can be fascinating and mysterious, possibly the last bastions of solitude in our fast-paced world. Just offshore the hub-bub and din of downtown Boston are some 17 deserted weed-covered islands, all steeped in intriguing history, seldom visited by residents of Beantown. Some, like Castle Island and George's Island, hold the ruins of bygone days, and are ripe with tales and legends of ghosts and things that go bump in the night.

I had the pleasure, if you want to call it that, of staying overnight at George's Island on the eve of the arrival of the Tall Ships to Boston Harbor in 1976. The experience was quite unsettling. Much of the island is covered with the well-preserved ruins of Fort Warren, an active fortress of the Civil War and prison for captured Rebel soldiers. Many of its dank, dark passages, rooms, and tunnels can be explored today, but some, because of dilapidated conditions, are closed off to public exploration. Thickets, creepers and prickly-bushes crowd the thick granite, crumbling brick walls and cubicles of the fort, giving the massive edifice an ancient, haunting look during the day, and a shadowy evil appearance at night. Once the sun goes down at George's Island, no one dares to leave the dock area to explore the fort. The island caretaker told me that night visits to the fort are not allowed because of the potential of someone tripping or falling and hurting themselves. But the real reason is that the ghost of the Black Widow walks the fort parapets, corridors and dungeons when the moon is high.

Legend has it that she came to Hull, Massachusetts in May of 1862, and admitted to a few residents there that her husband was a Confederate naval lieutenant, being held prisoner at Fort Warren. She was from South Carolina, and her accent was unmistakable, but because of her love for and devotion to her husband, the townfolks treated her with respect. One windy wet evening, she attempted the near-impossible—to free her husband from the prison. Dressed like a man, she confiscated a rowboat at Windmill Point in Hull, and rowed the one mile into the harbor to George's Island. Hiding the boat and avoiding the Yankee sentries, she made it to the fort, and began the herculean task of trying to dig under the ten-foot thick walls with a shovel she had brought along. Her husband, with the help of other inmates, had began tunneling through from the inside. Alert guards patrolling the island heard the scraping sounds, investigated, and found her engrossed in her work. Her husband was also discovered in the tunnel on the opposite side of the wall. Yankee Colonel Dimmick, the commander in charge of Fort Warren, confronted the two potential escapees, and was shocked when he realized that one was a woman. He was further surprised when she drew a pistol from her pant pocket and threatened to kill the colonel if he didn't let her and her husband go. A sentry lunged for the gun and she fired. The gun misfired, burning her hands and sending the musket-ball through her husband's chest, killing him instantly. She began screeching and wailing from that moment until the day of her hanging at Fort Warren, some five weeks later. Her only request being that she be allowed to wear women's clothes of mourning at her execution. After killing her husband, she welcomed death. The soldiers, both Yankee and Confederate, however, thought the colonel should spare her life, but their pleadings fell on deaf ears.

It was soon after she was hanged that guards and prisoners alike began spotting her night after night, floating along the parapets, or strolling the corridors, dressed in the black gown of a widow, and wearing a black veil or handkerchief, hiding much of her pale, white face. Sometimes soldiers reported they heard her weeping and wailing, not just during the Civil War, but throughout World War I and World War II, when small detachments of soldiers were stationed at the fort as part of Boston's harbor defenses. Many reports filtered into the mainland about the Lady In Black, or the Black Widow, as they often called her, being seen at Fort Warren, frightening soldiers half out of their wits. She is there alright, and her grave is there too, for all visitors to see.

About one and one half miles away, inland, and within sight of George's Island and the grave of the Black Widow, is Long Island. It also claims a female ghost connected with the Revolutionary War. She is The Woman In Red, also known as The Scarlet Woman. Her name was Mary Burton. With her husband William, she was escaping Boston with the British Army on March 17, 1776—Evacuation Day. Over 170 British ships were setting sail out of Boston Harbor, bound for Halifax, as George Washington's cannons bombarded them from Dorchester Heights. Aboard were some 9,000 British soldiers and over 3,000 Tories—civilian Americans who had decided to join with England in America's War For Independence. Aboard the ship MARGARET were the Burtons; he a dedicated servant of King George; she a more reluctant one. Mary hated to leave her beloved Boston, and as fate would have it, even though her ship was sailing out of the harbor, she would never leave. Standing on deck in a striking scarlet dress, a cannonball grazed the ship's rigging, and a dagger-like splinter of wood from the mast speared her head. She fell to the deck in a swoon. At first William thought she had just fainted, but then he saw the blood streaking through her hair and staining her dress. She opened her eyes for only a moment, and her final words to her husband were to plead that he bury her in Boston where she had lived all her life. He promised, as Mary died in his arms.

The captain of the MARGARET was reluctant to anchor off one of the harbor islands while the passengers performed a funeral ceremony. He suggested that Mary be buried at sea, but William Burton insisted that she be buried on the closest island, which happened to be Long Island. The ship's carpenter quickly whittled a wooden headstone for Mary, and a longboat put out for the island with the body of Mary aboard. The grave was dug, prayers were said, and Mary was buried, wrapped in canvas, with the wooden marker wedged into the rocky earth about her: *"Mary Burton 1748-1776."* The MARGARET sailed on to Halifax with William Burton aboard. He never returned to Boston again. The wooden marker soon rotted away, and today, nobody knows exactly where Mary Burton was buried. Legend has it that her remains lie at the brow of the hill near the ruins of Fort Strong, for this is where visitors to the island have seen her ghost on foggy and stormy evenings since September 1804. It was there and then that fishermen, seeking shelter from a terrible storm, camped within the crumbling walls at the fort, and first heard her moanings. Then they saw her apparition, *"a ghostly female form dressed in red,"* said one fisherman. She has been seen and heard periodically since then, but only in the evening during stormy weather. Private William Liddell, stationed at Long Island in 1891 as a sentry, reported seeing the woman in scarlet. *"She came towards me from the easterly,"* he said, *"over the hill by the fort, and her moaning and wailing were quite distinct."* The men building the bridge that now connects Long Island with the mainland at Squantum, also reported seeing *"the Lady In Red,"* in the Summer of 1951 during a heavy rain-squall. *"It wasn't my imagination,"* said laborer Jack Labrie. *"Five or six of us saw her just about sunset, trembling like a mirage, all in red, like she was glowing and on fire, but she had long yellowish hair, and drifted across the hill, like she was on a mission of some sort. She was about fifty yards away from us, and I wasn't scared or nothing, but thought it to be an interesting experience. I never saw another ghost before or since."* Whether the connecting bridge has allowed Mary to cross over to her beloved Boston, we'll never know, but I know of no ghostly sightings at Long Island since 1951.

The next island in towards Boston from Long Island, now also connected to the mainland, is Castle Island. Some two miles away from Long Island, it also houses a famous fort, Fort Independence, and is home to a notorious ghost. It, unlike the others, is not black, scarlet, or female—it is Green—Captain Robert F. Green of the United States Army. In life, he was a hateful, bullying man, and apparently is not friendly as a ghost, either. He was stationed at Castle Island in 1817, a barbaric officer, feared by his men, who tormented and teased anyone he didn't like into dueling him. Using either swords or pistols, he'd kill them, for he was an expert with both weapons. There was no penalty for his premeditated murders, for dueling, although scorned in the military, was legal then.

By Christmas Eve of 1817, Captain Green had already killed six men. That blustery evening, playing poker with eight fellow officers in their cozy quarters inside Fort Independence, Green, intoxicated, accused one of the players, Lieutenant Robert Massie, of cheating. The lieutenant insisted that he wasn't cheating, but Green slapped him across the face and challenged him to a duel. Massie accepted the challenge and swords were his weapons of choice, which pleased Green, for he was a master swordsman. Friends of Massie's tried to have Green call off the fight, slated for Dawn the next day. Massie refused. The experienced Captain Green easily pinned the lieutenant with his sword within a few minutes, and as eye witnesses vehmently protested, Green slashed Massie's throat with the tip of his dueling sword. After the burial of Lieutenant Massie on Christmas Day, his friends erected a marble monument which stands on the parade ground at Castle Island to this day. It reads: "Lt. Robert F. Massie—U.S. Regt. of Light Artillery—Here, 25th Dec. 1817, fell Lieut. Massie, aged 21." The strange aftermath of the duel was that a few weeks later, Captain Green disappeared from Fort Independence and was never seen again. Some of the soldiers thought he had deserted, but most knew better. Captain Green's home was the Army. He wouldn't leave it without a word to anyone. What then, many wondered, had happened to Captain Green?

The rumor of what happened to Captain Green was revealed to a teenaged private stationed at Castle Island ten years later. This Boston born youth had enlisted in the Army only a few weeks before his assignment as sentry at Fort Independence, under the alias, Edgar M. Perry. He was told that the ghost of Captain Green, wearing tattered uniform and wielding his sword, walked the ramparts of the old fort during the cold winter nights, searching for someone to challenge to a duel. Perry even thought he saw the specter of the captain one snowy evening. But, he was more interested in finding out what had happened to Green to suddenly convert him into an angry ghost. Sworn to secrecy, the inquisitive Perry was told by his commanding officer that the friends of Lieutenant Massie proceeded to get Captain Green intoxicated one night soon after New Year's, 1818. Green, loving his whiskey and rum as much as a fight, was lured into a subterrainian dungeon on the pretext that a duel between two other officers would take place there that evening. Once in the dimly lit dungeon, one officer clubbed Green and two others shackled him to the wall, cuffing him hand and foot. A fourth conspirator began bricking up the wall using mortar, freshly mixed for the occasion. The quartet of officers managed to build a wall, neck high around Captain Green. When he regained consciousness, a cloth soaked with rum was stuffed into his mouth. His four fellow officers, all friends of Lieutenant Massie, stood before the stunned captain, saluted him, then bricked up the rest of wall to the ceiling. Captain Green died a slow painful death, his grieving moans echoing behind the brick wall, but never heard in the fort above.

Perry didn't know whether to believe the story or not, but after his tour of duty, and a short stint at West Point, he decided to write about what had happened to Captain Green. His fictionalized story, "The Cask of Amontillado," became a best seller, and in fact prompted the elders of Boston to name an alley downtown after him—not *"Perry Alley,"* but *"Poe Alley,"* for Perry's real name was Edgar Allan Poe. The truth of what happened to Captain Green was revealed in 1905, 56 years after Poe's death. Six Boston laborers, in the process of repairing the underpinnings of Fort Independence, broke through a brick wall and there in lantern light came face to face with a skeleton wearing a ragged red uniform, shackled to a dungeon wall, a dusty cloth still stuffed into its mouth. The body, of course, could not be identified, but everyone who had read Edgar Allen Poe's story, knew who it was. The skeleton was given a proper burial on Castle Island in 1905, but Captain Green is still seen from time to time, in ghostly form, tramping the parapet overlooking Boston harbor usually on snowy nights around Christmas.

These are the ghosts of the harbor, a colorful trio of black, red and Green, all awaiting your visit to their ruined fortresses, only a stone's throw from the skyscrapers of downtown Boston.

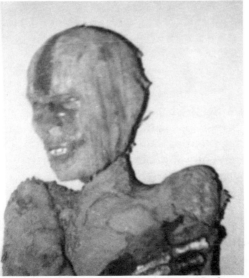

The evil Captain Green of Castle Island, Boston Harbor, was sealed into a dungeon under Fort Independence in 1818, and uncovered by workmen in 1905. He now haunts the island.

VII
Phantom Ships

Australians Roger and Ann Dowling and their two teenaged sons, Jon and Mark, were sailing around the world in their 32-foot sloop SHANA. By August of 1983, they were off the east coast of America, heading for Bermuda. *"We were becalmed for two days,"* Roger later reported to Dick Donavan of the *Weekly World News, "and we were surrounded by a dense white fog. What bothered me the most however,"* said Dowling, *"was that my compass was acting strange. It just kept swinging from one point to the other, I had no idea where we were. I couldn't get the engine started and my radio was on the blink."* At twilight of the third day, with his wife and sons sleeping in the cabin below, Roger was sitting on deck, dozing at the helm, when he saw something sail out of the fog and cross the bow of his sloop. *"I watched in horror as an ancient man-of-war lifted out of the sea,"* he said. *"I rubbed my eyes, thinking I was dreaming. It was carrying tattered sails, and worn battle-flags were flying from the mast-head, but the hulk itself was hardly moving. I called to my wife and the boys to come on deck quick, and when they saw the old moss covered ship, stark terror flooded their eyes."*

"I just screamed," reported Anna Dowling. *"I've never known such icy fear in all my life. There were horrid silent corpses, motionless, but staring down at us from the rail."*

"Then, without so much as a whisper of a sound," said Roger, *"the phantom-ship just sank out of sight. There wasn't even a ripple in the water. It just vanished. Almost at once, the haze lifted, the compass settled down and the wind picked up. I didn't even ask the others if they wanted to head on to Bermuda. I just turned the SHANA around and headed for the nearest American port."*

Were the Dowlings lying, possibly to gain publicity? Or maybe they suffered from a mass-hallucination? It may have been another vessel passing close by through the fog-bank, giving the impression to the Dowlings of a battle worn man-of-war of centuries past. Whatever it was, the bizzare sighting was enough for the Dowlings to give up their plan to sail the Atlantic Ocean to England. All four had been deeply frightened and were still visibly shaking when they reached port later that day. Sailors becalmed or lost at sea have been known to hallucinate, seeing things or people in perfect form who just weren't there, but never have I heard of four people having the same hallucination at the same time! The skeptic must then conclude that it was a real ship, or that light refraction in some way caused the fog to take the shape of an ancient vessel. Their story is hard to believe, yet many others down through the ages have experienced the same thing. Old superstitious fishermen and mariners, who often returned from a voyage with tales of sighting a phantom ship, thought that such sightings meant impending doom or death. There are probably more phantom vessels spotted off New England's rugged coast than anywhere in the world, and most are during storms or when a dense fog hangs over the sea. The confluence of the cold waters of the Labrador Current meeting the warm waters of the Gulf Stream offshore, make New England the foggiest place in the world, and like sleds coming out in a snowstorm, phantom ships usually appear when New England is blanketed with thick fog.

The Puritans who settled at Salem, Massachusetts in 1630, recorded the periodic sighting of a *"spectre ship"* or *"spiritual rover of surrounding sea"* that sailed backwards, with only one man and one woman on deck, presumedly lovers, sailing the seas 'til the end of time, in reverse. The famous Puritan minister Cotton Mather, in his book *"Magnolia Christi,"* writes of another phantom ship seen by many in the harbor at New Haven, Connecticut in 1647. *"There being yet living so many credible gentlemen,"* wrote Mather, *"that were eyewitness to this wonderful thing, I venture to publish it for a thing as undoubted as it is wonderful."*

One of these witnesses was James Pierpont of New Haven. *"A new ship, built at Rhode Island, of about 150 tons,"* he reported, *"departed for London, England, in January, cutting her way through much ice,"* before clearing the Sound and heading out into the Atlantic. In a letter to Mather, Pierpont writes that the master of the vessel, Lamberton, felt the ship, laden with rich cargo and wealthy passengers, *"was so walty, that she would prove their grave."* Unfortunately Lamberton was aboard when his prediction of doom was realized. The ship disappeared, never reaching England and never returning to her home port. Suspecting the worst, a day of prayer for the ship and passengers was held at New Haven in April. *"If it be the Lord's pleasure,"* cried Reverend Davenport from the pulpit, *"let us hear what He has done with our dear friends."* Some six weeks later, in early June, before sunset and after a thunderstorm, a ship under sail with flags flying was spotted coming up the harbor. Word quickly spread through the port town that Lamberton's vessel was coming in, and all rushed to the dock to greet her.

"Seemingly with her sails filled under a fresh gale," wrote Pierpont, *"holding her course north, she continued under observation, sailing against the wind for a space of half an hour. Many were drawn to behold this great work of God; yea, the very children cryed out, 'There's a brave ship!'....The vessel came so near some of the spectators, as that they imagined a man might*

hurl a stone on board her, her main-top seemed to be blown off, but left hanging in the shrouds; then her mizzen-top; then all her masting seemed blown away by the board: quickly after the hulk brought unto a careen, she overset, and so vanished into a smoky cloud...."

Some of the witnesses, including Reverend Davenport, saw a man on deck pointing a sword out to sea, and all reported seeing the *"spectre ship"* sink before their eyes. *"This was the very mould of our ship,"* Reverend Davenport announced to the spellbound citizens at dockside, *"and thus was her tragic end. God has condescended for the quieting of afflicted spirits."*

"...And at last their prayers were answered;
It was in the month of June,
An hour before the Sunset
On a windy afternoon,
When, steadily steering landward,
A ship was seen below,
And they knew it was Lamberton, Master,
Who sailed so long ago...."
From the poem: "Phantom Ship"
By Henry Wadsworth Longfellow

Although James Pierpont and Cotton Mather both mention that Connecticut's phantom ship was built in Rhode Island before its brief resurrection, Rhode Islanders are more obsessed with a phantom ship that appears from time to time off their own coast. And another famous poet, John Greenleaf Whittier, adds credence to these sightings;

"....Down swooped the wreckers, like birds of prey
Tearing the heart of the ship away,
And the dead had never a word to say.
And then, with ghastly shimmer and shine
Over the rocks and the seething brine,
They burned the wreck of the 'Palatine."
....Behold! again, with shimmer and shine,
Over the rocks and the seething brine,
The flaming wreck of the 'Palatine!' ...."

Since before the Revolutionary War the burning phantom ship, considered to be either the square-rigger PALATINE or the bark PRINCESS AUGUSTA, has been spotted every other year between Christmas and New

Year's Day between Block Island and the mainland of Rhode Island. Ben Cogdon in the year 1800, wrote, *"I have seen her eight or ten times or more. In those early days nobody doubted her being sent by an Almighty Power...We lived, when I was young, in Charlestown, directly opposite Block Island, where we used to have a plain view of the burning ship."* Some eighty years later, Rowland Robinson of Narragansett, Rhode Island, wrote in his *"Recollections Of Olden Times,"* that *"George Sheffield and Shedrick Card, two venerable old patriarchs, both of whom were very intelligent, neither had the least doubt of their having seen the ship all in flames, and that her bona-fide appearance was no more than an ordinary occurrence."* Another 19th century recollection was that an old man living at Block Island, *"always became madly insane after Christmas, and would rave about seeing a ship all ablaze, with men falling from her burning rigging and shrouds."*

There have been countless reports of sightings throughout this century, and in 1940 they were so numerous that the Coast Guard patrolled the seaboard in an attempt to confront the phantom ship. Coast Guard officials concluded that the many eye-witnesses were seeing only *"natural phosphorescence."* Another heavy surge of sightings occurred in 1969, when excited and often frightened Rhode Islanders swore they saw not only the PALATINE ablaze, but the spectre of a young woman on deck with something in her hands she was attempting to throw into the ocean. Again, the Coast Guard was called out to search the seas but did not encounter any burning vessel.

The PRINCESS AUGUSTA wrecked off Block Island on the day after Christmas in 1738. Aboard were 360 emigrants from Rotterdam, Holland, most of them sick or dying from drinking contaminated water. When the bark hit the rocks, rescue boats headed out from the island, but the sea was rough and the passengers had little energy to assist the islanders in boarding the doomed ship. In an attempt to either keep warm or to signal the islanders, a fire was lit on deck, and soon the ship was ablaze. A strong change of wind lifted her off the rocks and she sailed back out to sea, outdistancing her rescuers who could only watch her burn to the waterline and sink. Many believe it is the PRINCESS AUGUSTA and not the PALATINE that is still seen blazing off Block Island, searching for a port to deposit her Rotterdam refugees. Whittier's poem has convinced most that the phantom ship is the PALATINE, but Block Islanders refute the poet's claim that their ancestors were wreckers. *"May God forgive the hands that fed, the false lights over the rocky Head!"* Was this poetic license on Whittier's part, or did wicked islanders actually cause the PALATINE to wreck?

Some island historians write that the PALATINE only touched shore at Block Island to let off sick passengers, and then sailed on to Philadelphia. On shore at Sandy Point there are four graves of PALATINE passengers and a monument that tells a different story. The vessel, carrying German emigrants from Palatinates, burned to the waterline and sank offshore, two days after Christmas of 1752. The motley PALATINE crew mutinied, threw the captain overboard, robbed the passengers, torched the ship and escaped in longboats. Seeing the vessel ablaze offshore, Block Island fishermen tried to save as many passengers as possible. Many were frightened and jumped into the frigid sea to drown, some others burned to death. One demented woman refused to be rescued and remained on board to go down with the ship. There were few survivors. One was *"Old Dutch Chrissy,"* who decided to live in a shack on Block Island near the wreck site. She became a local witch, and the place where she made her home to this day is called *"Haunted Field." "Nothing will grow in that field,"* islanders will tell you, *"for Dutch Chrissy left a curse on it."* If islanders didn't cause the PALATINE to wreck, one wonders why this witchy survivor left a curse on them. And why have islanders for over two centuries seen this burning ghost-ship off their coast?

The famous fishing port of Gloucester, Massachusetts would be remiss if she didn't have a phantom ship. Her story has also been preserved in poetry, but unlike the PALATINE horror, the spectre ship ALICE MARR is a vision of love won and love lost. If one should see this haunted schooner bucking the waves in an attempt to make Gloucester Harbor, then, as the legend goes, he or she will lose the one they love most.

Alice Marr, a fisherman's daughter, was the most beautiful girl in town, loved by all the young men who tried in every way to win her heart. John Ackman went so far as to name his vessel after her. An old ballad written by Norman Gunnison tells us that, *"Lovers sought Alice from near and far,"* but she finally decided, *"she'd be John Ackman's promised bride."* John and Alice were to be married after his next fishing trip, and no happier man ever sailed out of Gloucester Harbor to the fishing banks than John Ackman aboard his ALICE MARR.

.... *"Months rolled on, and never a word;*
Six months, twelve months: on the day
That finished the year, was a rumour heard
Of the Alice Marr in the outer bay.
Boats put out, but they drew not near,
Slowly, silently, on she steered:
"Skipper Ackman! Ho! What cheer?"
She had vanished, had disappeared.
Fisherman, tell me why yonder boat

Sails, and no nearer comes to shore;
Nor a ripple her bow breaks o'er?
"Stranger, I reckon you aren't here long;
Many a year her pennant flew.
Old is the story; a worn-out song,
But her deck is trod by no mortal crew...."

The beautiful Alice Marr never married, but was often seen roaming the high cliffs overlooking the ocean near the mouth of Gloucester Harbor, awaiting John's return. On the twilight of every New Year's Eve, the schooner ALICE MARR is seen under full sail heading into the harbor but disappears before making port.

Phantom ships seem to hold a special attraction for poets. It was John Greenleaf Whittier again who penned the lines:

"What makes thee in the haunts of home,
A wonder and a sign?
No foot is on thy silent deck,
Upon the helm no hand,
No ripple hath the soundless wind,
That smites thee from the land!"

In his *"Dead Ship of Harpswell,"* Whittier was intrigued with the many sightings in Casco Bay, Maine, of a full-rigged sailing ship seen on foggy mornings and evenings, sailing into Harpswell and disappearing before she reached port. In 1880, the phantom ship was seen by over thirty guests at the Harpswell House that faces the bay, and she has been spotted now and then, well into the 1980s. She is said to be the SARAH, that like the ALICE MARR, was named for a pretty teenaged girl who was betrothed to a local sea captain, George Leverett. The first mate of Leverett's merchant ship, Charles Jose, also loved Sarah Soule of Freeport, and when Sarah agreed to marry Leverett, Charles Jose was enraged. He quit his post aboard the SARAH and swore revenge. Becoming a pirate in the winter of 1812, Jose persuaded a Spanish captain and crew to pursue the SARAH from Maine to Nassau, and there, attack and plunder her. The pirate crew of the SALAZAR boarded the SARAH and killed everyone on board but George Leverett. Jose had the Spaniards lash him to the mast, then hoist the sails of the SARAH. Jose and the Spaniards then sailed away in the SALAZAR, watching the SARAH, with Leverett tied securely to the mast, catch the wind and head north never to be seen again. When the fog rolls in over Harpswell, at Dawn or Dusk, the SARAH, now with tattered sails and a corpse lashed to the mast, attempts to make port, but never quite makes it.

Like the famed FLYING DUTCHMAN, New England's spiritual rovers of the sea have been seen by sailors and landlubbers as well, reaping the wild wind and struggling through the fog in endless, vain attempts to reach port. Are they merely figments of the imagination? Fearful sailors who have sworn oaths that they have seen Phantom Ships, vehemently proclaim their existence, and that they are harbingers of doom. King James VI wrote that Phantom Ships were caused by, *"witches, that can raise storms and tempests in the salt air, either on land or sea."* No one, it seems, can explain this phenomenon, but there is little doubt that, like the FLYING DUTCHMAN, they will be with us 'til doomsday.

VIII
Werewolves And Witches Of Dogtown

Overlooking Gloucester, Rockport and Ipswich Bay is a thickly wooded rock-strewn plateau called Dogtown. It was once a thriving community of over 100 families, but now it's a ghost town, overgrown with shrubs and briar-patches, with not even the visible remains of a cellarhole. Like any deserted village, tales of Dogtown are replete with ghosts, witches and wild animals. The difference here is that there are many unique facts and unusual bits of evidence to substantiate the legends. It is said that Dogtown was a village filled with witches, and there is no doubt about this. Many openly practiced the Black Arts here, and at one time, only witches lived in Dogtown. From pre-revolutionary War days to well into the 19th century, it was mainly a community of old crones, widows of Gloucester fishermen and soldiers lost at sea or in the wars, who became soothsayers and fortune tellers in their efforts to survive. They acquired dogs as protection form outside intruders, and thus were given the name, *"Dogtowners"* The many dogs, underfed and unkempt, ran wild, stimulating talk in the surrounding towns that on the nights of a full moon, many of the witches of Dogtown turned into werewolves.

A werewolf, of course, is more fearsome than a wolf, a timber-wolf, or even a pack of wolves, for it is really a human that transforms into a ferocious beast with furry coat, hairy claw-like hands and feet, and fang-like teeth. It prowls and attacks only on the full moon, using both fangs and claws to rip open its victim's throat, tearing out the heart, but otherwise not disfiguring the victim in any other way, be it man or animal. Legend has it, that the only way to kill a werewolf is by firing a silver bullet through its heart. All this would seem a bit far-fetched, even silly, if it weren't for the fact that some strange vicious creature stalked the woods of Dogtown through the years, attacking dogs, deer, cows, horses, and humans with wild abandon, only when the moon was full. And that same, or a similar creature, is on the prowl in the vicinity of Dogtown to this very day.

First mention of Dogtown witches being able to change themselves into creatures of their choosing, comes in the popular Gloucester legend about the witch *"Old Meg."* When the young men of Gloucester volunteered to join other New Englanders in the siege of Louisburg at Nova Scotia in 1745, toothless Old Meg, whose real name was Margaret Wesson, was at the dock to see them off to war. As excited and nervous as they were, Old Meg didn't soothe their nerves, standing there cackling at them as they boarded the vessel that would transport them to the French fortress at Cape Breton. The attack was successful, but one day, soon after the battle, two of the Gloucester lads of Captain Byles' company, spied a large crow flying over the captured fort. It hovered over them for hours.

It was well known in Gloucester Towne that Old Meg loved transforming herself into either a wolf or a crow, and the cry of the bird that seemed to be hounding them at Nova Scotia, sounded much like the mocking cackle from Meg when they were leaving port. One of the boys threw a rock at the crow and nearly hit it, but then it started diving down at them, screeching just like the old Dogtown witch, and forcing them to take cover. Realizing that only a silver bullet could kill the likes of Old Meg, they molded a bullet from a silver button taken from a uniform, loaded it into a musket and shot the crow. It was hit in the leg and fell to the ground, but managed to fly off again before the boys could kill it. Returning home two weeks later, they were told that Old Meg was dying, bedridden with a fractured leg she sustained in a fall two weeks earlier. The wound had festered and the infection killed her only a few days after the troops had returned to Gloucester victorious. Old Doctor Gregs reported after the witch was buried, that he had found a silver sleeve button deeply imbedded in her infected leg wound. Gloucester's Revolutionary Colonel William Pearce, who was also a Dogtowner said that *"Meg Wesson was the only reputed witch of Cape Ann of whom it can be alleged, with history to endorse the allegation, that she rode on a broomstick."*

It is obvious from this tale, originating over fifty years after the Salem witch hysteria, that superstitions and fear of witches still dominated New England culture well into the eighteenth century. Over a century later, Newbury's Sarah Anna Emery, in her book *"Reminiscences Of A Nonagenarian,"* relates an episode that further stimulated old fears and superstitions and enhanced the werewolf legend of Dogtown.

"Dogtown was two miles distant from Crane-neck," wrote Ms. Emery in about the year 1879, even then referring to Dogtown as a place that *"Was." "After passing Dale's Pond, the road ran through thick woods. This, on some dark and stormy nights, was rather bug-a-booish, and on one occasion old Amos Pillsbury got a terrible scare from which he never became wholly relieved. We were at breakfast when he entered one morning, looking frightened and pale. The old man lisped slightly and said, 'Oh Mr. Smith I see a terrible critter in the woods beyont the pond last night....It was a terrible big critter, as big as Brindle's calf. It's eyes were like fire coals, and it ran past me through the bushes, about a rod from the road, with every hair whistling like a bell.'*

'It must have been the wolverine--my old granny used to keep us

young'uns quiet with stories about the wolverine out beyant in the woods. I used to be afeared to stir ten yards from the door o'nights; but, as I had never seen the critter afore, I had begun to think it was one of Granny's stories, but I seed him last night, sartin sure, and his eyes were like fire coals, and every hair whistled like a bell.'

The old man was so sure that the neighboring men turned out that night, each armed and equipped for a deadly encounter with some ferocious beast, but nothing was found; and though the quest was continued by the young men and boys for several evenings, no strange animal was ever discovered. But old Pillsbury, to his dying day, used to declare there was 'a wolverine in the woods,' and nothing could ever again induce the old man to travel the road alone after nightfall."

Dogtown was a place most people avoided anyway, even during its heyday, and with good reason. Children were petrified to go near this noted haven of witches, and only the brave, the foolish, and the very wild citizens of surrounding towns and villages, would venture into Dogtown after dark. Even today, although there is no sign of a human being ever having lived there, there is a foreboding, mysterious atmosphere about the place. Prickly bramble-bushes, tall black pines and enormous boulders that dwarf the thickets give the place an unearthly atmosphere. Each of these large chunks of granite has a name and a history to it. The white faced *"Split Rock"* is located on the edge of what once was the center of downtown Dogtown, called *"Dogtown Common."* It measures about 15 feet high by approximately 40 feet wide, and looks like a giant split tooth. It was coincidentally, where Dogtown's cobbler-dentist, Johnny Morgan Stanwood, who was crippled in the war of 1812, set up shop after the war. His *"booth built of slab and covered with turf,"* was still standing throughout the Civil War. Locals called his cobbler hut, *"The Boo,"* maybe because it was a frightening place. A cow once got caught in the crack in the center of the boulder, and although twenty farmers tried to pry her loose, she couldn't be budged, so she was slaughtered for steaks right there on the spot.

Not far from Split Rock is another massive boulder called *"Whale's Jaw,"* because it looks like the jutting jaw of a sperm whale. Here, one morning in 1814, Abraham Wharf, who lived in a house located only a few feet away from the boulder, walked there from his house with his razor and slit his own throat. *"Lonely and weary,"* writes Babson in his *"History of Gloucester," "he crawled under the rock and committed suicide."* Abraham's sister was wife of Peter Lurvey. He and Benjamin Rowe, were the two martyred heroes of the Battle of Fortpoint, Gloucester, when the Royal Marines of the British sloop FALCON on August 8, 1775, bombarded and then at-

- 43 -

tempted to attack the town. It was then they were driven back to their ship by the Gloucester fishermen and Lurvey was killed. Mrs. Lurvey lived on next to Whale's Jaw to the ripe old age of 104. She was Dogtown's oldest citizen.

Other glacial monstrosities of Dogtown are *"Pulpit Rock, Uncle Andrew's Rock"* and *"Whetstone Rock,"* the latter having, so Charles Mann tells us in his 1896 *"Story of Dogtown,"* *"a place hollowed out that was often used as a urinal."* Near Whetstone Rock is a ferny marsh filled with sumac known in the old days as *"Granny Day's Swamp,"* she being the local school marm. *"The swamp"*, says Mann, *"was always the repository of one or more unfortunates, which have got in but could never get out."*

The last resident to leave Dogtown was an African named Cornelius Finson, alias *"Black Neil,"* and he left reluctantly in February of 1830. Constable Tucker dragged him out of a cellarhole and took him off to the poor farm. Black Neil was suffering from malnutrition and had frostbitten toes and he lived for only one week at the poor farm. Some said that he had been bewitched by the crones of Dogtown when he was a young man. He had been a clerk for the Annisquam Fishing Company, but left his job to live in Dogtown, where he was convinced *"Old Molly Jakups (Jacobs) had hid a great treasure in the cellar of the Lurvey House."* He was still talking about the treasure when he was hauled off to the poor farm.

Molly Jacobs was *"an unsavory character,"* so Mann tells us, a practicing witch and fortune teller, full of cures and curses, for anyone who'd give her a penny or refuse to do so. Molly and her sister moved into the Lurvey house after Abraham Wharf committed suicide, to help care for Mrs. Lurvey and her grandson Sam Stanley, who they brought up as a girl. They survived on reading cards and coffee-grounds to any neighbor or stranger who wished to know his future. The roof went first, and snow sprinkled down into their bedrooms throughout the winter. Then one day, two of the Day boys came to take the house away, moving it to Washington Street, Gloucester. Molly, Mrs. Lurvey, and Sarah Jacobs Phipps, Molly's sister, went off to live in the poor house, and young Sam Stanley went off to Rockport to hire out as a washer woman. Why Black Neil stayed behind to scour the cellarhole for poor old Molly's treasure, only he knows.

Another who stayed with him until her house fell in and she died of malnutrition and exposure in 1830, was witch Judy Rhines (Ryan), also described in old town records as, *"an unsavory character."* Judy was also a notorious fortune teller, who had a freakish mouth deformity— *"she had teeth like a dog"*—better known as canines. Black Neil was described by Charles Mann as having, *"long teeth protruding from his upper lip;"* and

Old Tammy Younger, Dogtown's most noted witch, had *"two long teeth sticking out of her upper jaw,"* which she loved to curse through. It was Johnny Morgan Stanwood, so the story goes, who pulled Tammy Younger's two front teeth half way out at *"The Boo"* beneath Split Rock, but she cursed so at him for causing her pain that Johnny refused to finish the job, *"and he just left Tammy's teeth dangling in her mouth."* It's told that *"they jiggled considerably when she talked after that, and especially when she cursed."* No wonder it was thought that these bizarre villagers with fang-like teeth turned into werewolves at a full moon.

The short, chubby Tammy Younger and her ill-humored Aunt Lucey George were called the *"Princess and Queen of Fox Hill,"* a section of Dogtown overlooking the Annisquam River and Ipswich Bay, only a few hundred yards from the Common. Their home was *"a resort of bucanneers and lawless men,"* writes Mann, where there was not only a lot of card readings, but card playing as well. It became known in the early 19th century, as *"Tammy's Tavern,"* where *"Tammy's Viper,"* was the strongest drink sold. Tammy insisted that anyone coming up the Fox Hill Road stop to buy something from her, strong drink, berries she had picked, fire wood, bread she had baked, or whatever. If they weren't willing to buy anything from her, she'd confront them insisting that they give her a handout of whatever they were carrying on their carts, or possibly a coin or two. If they refused, she would verbally, toe to toe, bewitch them, or their animals, should they be on horseback or driving oxen. If they laughed or scoffed, and attempted to travel on over the hill without giving her anything, she would spit at them and follow them for a few steps, shouting profanity into their ears. As Mann tells us, *"she had a very choice vocabulary."* She died on February 4, 1829, at age 76. Soon after her death, a sizeable sum of money was found in the cellar of her house, which may be why Black Neil almost froze to death trying to uncover Molly Jackups supposed treasure in the cellarhole of the Lurvey house. Historian Charles Mann writes, *"a friend was, a few years since, chasing a woodchuck, which went into Tammy Younger's cellar. In digging for the animal he unearthed a handsomely ornamented snuff-box, the cover bearing a representation of a full-rigged ship. It was probably Tammy's, as she is said to have been a snuff taker as well as a smoker."*

For a community that lasted 169 years (1661 to 1830) it is amazing how many self proclaimed witches, whose fame or notoriety spread to towns miles away, came from the village of Dogtown. Patience Hope, a lovely name for a witch, was considered one of the better fortune tellers, as was Becky Rich, who was supposedly adept at reading tea leaves. Her mother Rachel read only coffee grounds, and would only tell the fortunes of children. *"Old Ruth,"* a mulatto ex-slave, lived with the Riches. She dressed like a man, always doing man's work, and was known in Gloucester and Rockport as *"John Woodman—stone mason."* Gloucester poet Hiram Rich, once commented, *"Aunt Becky was a nice old woman, but little reliance was placed on her fortunes."* He also remarked, *"John Woodman died in the poor house, wearing a skirt."* Living across the road from the Riches, were the Days, one of whom, Issac Day, was a cannoneer aboard the U.S.S. CONSTITUTION, *"Old Ironsides,"* but his sister, the old Dogtown school teacher, was considered a witch, especially by the children of Dogtown. She was, however, considered a good witch, concocting various cures and love potions from the leaves, herbs, berries and flowers growing in and around Dogtown. She came from a family that produced three sets of twins, so local folks took great stock in her potions.

"Old Chap Houghty," another Dogtown school teacher witch, was famous for her codfish-turnip stew, with periwinkles added, which everyone knew cured any and all aches of the body, *"especially those of the limbjoints."* Another who was famous for her medicinal cures was *"Daffy Archer,"* she made her home brewed *"water-tonic,"* from the mucous of snails. She also constantly wore around her neck, in keeping with Dogtown legend, the three-inch fang of a wolf. Another witch *"Aunt Rachel,"* brewed a potent concoction which she sold in the towns, made of foxberry leaves and thought to be *"a dire drink."* It is said to have driven Aunt Rachel's neighbor Molly Miller insane, and *"she had to be tied up in her room."* Aunt Rachel's son, Jack Smith, killed himself one night in the house, and rumor was, it was just after Aunt Rachel had brewed a new batch of her foxberry leaves and had tested its potency on young Jack. Standing near Rachel Smith's home was the Tucker house. Dorcas Tucker also dabbled with herbs and various concoctions in her kitchen cauldron. She was called *"Dark Tucker,"* but called herself, *"The Nurse."*

Another noted local witch was Molly Stevens, also known as *"Joe Stevens,"* and often called, *"a pain in the butt,"* by villagers, for she was always fighting and shouting and loudly boasting to others of her grand abilities as a fortune teller. Probably the wisest witch of the Dogtown lot, was an English woman named Esther *"Easter"* Carter. Molly Joe Stevens especially didn't like her witch neighbor because she was smart and was English, not a popular nationality after the War of 1812, which was about the time Easter came to Dogtown. Easter also put on aristocratic airs, although she was very poor. *"I shall not subsist on berries like Molly Stevens,"* she told those who visited her for future visions, *"for I eats no trash."* What she did subsist on was cabbage, which was about the only vegetable that grew well in Dogtown. Easter's house always smelled of boiling cabbage, which she would freely offer to anyone who would join her for lunch or supper.

The constant smell of it in her humble home kept many potential customers away. This was unfortunate, for her intuitive guesses of a person's future were better than those of any of the soothsayers of Dogtown. She was also a respected healer.

If the mile or so of winding dirt paths from Gloucester or Rockport, up the craggy plateau of high granite ledges to Dogtown is taken, one will see a set of round boulders on the south side of Dogtown Road. On one, neatly chiseled are the words: *"First Attack;"* and on the other, *"James Merry died, Sept. 10, 1892."* Walking on into the thorny overgrown field that was once Dogtown Common, you'll come upon other boulders with sayings carved into them, such as: *"Be On Time,"* or *"Help Mother,"* or, *"Get a Job,"* seemingly messages to the long gone inhabitants of the village, who, near the end of their days at Dogtown, were considered shirkers and misfits by the people of Gloucester and Rockport. Actually the latter rock carvings were done by Roger Babson, the owner of Dogtown in 1929-30, who bequeathed the land to Gloucester as a public park, apparently hoping his expertly carved slogans would have an effect on idle teenagers, who he hoped would use the park as a hangout. The *"First Attack"* and the *"James Merry"* carvings were made by Raymond Tarr in the late 1800s, marking the location of New England's one and only bullfight, and the death of the toreodor, James Merry.

Merry, a giant of a man, six feet seven inches tall, and weighing over 250 pounds, was a mariner who had traveled the world and was intrigued with the bullfights he had witnessed in Spain. A young bull was pastured on the road to Dogtown, and on a wager from his drinking buddies, they all went up to Dogtown from Gloucester center to watch James taunt, tease and then successfully wrestle the bull to the ground. He returned to the pasture a year later, supposedly alone, to fight the bull again. He was later found dead in the pasture, gored to death, with a deep wound in his neck. Most believed that the bull, now bigger and stronger, had won this second fight. Others of his friends who had seen the bloody gash in Merry's throat, believed it was some other animal that killed him on September 10, 1892. Even though the witches of Dogtown had deserted the village some sixty years earlier, Merry had been killed on the night of a full moon, and folks insisted that werewolves still prowled the area.

The Agawam Indians, who often visited the Dogtown area in the late summer and fall, came to get their fill of luscious raspberries, blackberries, and blueberries. The berries have been available in abundance here, especially in and around Brier Swamp, since before the White Man came. These same Indians believed that their ancestors had heads like dogs. The Indians also thought that if anyone ate the wolfbane plant, hair would grow on their face, claws would grow from their fingers, and they would assume the features of their dog-like ancestors. Possibly, this is where the initial werewolf legend of Dogtown found its inspiration and was passed on from generation to generation by the superstitious fishermen and mariners of Gloucester and Rockport. Also, when the English and Welch fishermen settled at Cape Ann, some three years before the Pilgrims arrived at Plymouth on the MAYFLOWER, they were plagued by ravaging wolves, who often attacked their settlement for a portion of their fish catch. The wolves dens were in the highlands overlooking Gloucester, a mile or two from the sea, and this also may have prompted the assumption that werewolves lived in the upland, which soon was to be known as Dogtown.

On March 17, 1984, at about six p.m., just as the full moon was rising over the dunes across the Annisquam at Crane's Beach Reservation, David Myska saw a large beastly creature roaming the highland cliffs above the dunes. *"It was a very large dog or cat,"* David, who is from Allston, Massachusetts, reported to Ipswich police, *"possibly a mountain lion."* Wayne Milton, the supervisor of the Crane Reservation, didn't think it was a mountain lion, for such an animal hadn't been seen in Eastern Massachusetts for two hundred years. Harry Leno, the Ipswich animal control officer also said that he doubted it was a mountain lion, and thought it might be a coy-dog, combination wolf and coyote, a new breed of wild animal making its way into New Hampshire and Maine through Canada. David Myska said *"the animal is too big to be a wolf or coyote."* A strange huge animal was also spotted at nearby Rowley, a few nights later.

Four nights later, one of the many deer that wander Crane's Beach Reservation, was found dead, its throat slashed, with deep fang marks in its neck and chest. *"It was horribly mutilated,"* reported Harry Leno. *"Yet no part of it had been eaten."* Whatever the animal was that attacked and killed the deer, it did not do so for food, otherwise the deer would have been found partially eaten. *"It was an animal thirsting for blood."* Harry Leno believed it was a large dog, or maybe a pack of dogs, or possibly even a large wolf. *"Anything is possible,"* he concluded. That same evening across the Annisquam at Raynard Street, two teenagers in a car reported sighting *"a gray monstrous dog-like animal, running into the woods. It had big teeth and was foaming at the mouth."* Nothing was seen or heard of it again. Only the people who live on Raynard Street remain a bit squeamish about the sighting of this strange animal. For, you see, Raynard Street leads into Dogtown, and Dogtown overlooks Crane's Beach Reservation, and well, as Harry Leno says, *"anything is possible."*